NATURE'S FURY

BLIZZARDS

Cari Meister

ABDO
& Daughters

Visit us at
www.abdopub.com

Published by ABDO Publishing Company, 4940 Viking Drive, Edina, MN 55435.
Copyright ©1999 by Abdo Consulting Group, Inc. International copyrights reserved in all countries. No part of this book may be reproduced in any form without written permission from the publisher.

Printed in the United States.

Edited by: Paul Joseph
Art Direction: John Hamilton
Contributing Editor: Morgan Hughes

Cover photo: AP/Wide World Photos
Interior photos: Digital Stock, pages 1, 27, 31
          Corbis, pages 2, 4-15, 17, 20, 21, 23, 25, 28
          National Weather Service, page 16

Sources: Dennis, Jerry. *It's Raining Frogs and Fishes: Four Seasons of Natural Phenomena and Oddities of the Sky.* New York: HarperCollins Publishers, 1992; Kahl, Jonathan D.W. *Weather Watch: Forecasting the Weather.* Minneapolis: Lerner Publications Company, 1996; Laskin, David. *Braving the Elements: The Stormy History of American Weather.* New York: Doubleday, 1996; Stonehouse, Bernard. *Snow, Ice and Cold.* New York: New Discovery Books, 1992; Various articles on http://weathereye.kgan.com; Various articles on http://www.usatoday.com; *Wonders of Weather: Snow.* New York: Ambrose Video Publishing Inc, 1995.

Library of Congress Cataloging–in–Publication Data

Meister, Cari.
    Blizzards / Cari Meister
        p. cm. — (Nature's fury)
    Includes bibliographical references and index.
    Summary: Discusses the nature, causes, and dangers of blizzards, blizzards of the past, and ways to survive them.
    ISBN 1-57765-085-9
    1. Blizzards—Juvenile literature. [1. Blizzards] I. Title. II. Series: Meister, Cari. Nature's fury.
QC926.37.M45   1999
551.55 '5—DC21
                                        98-11989
                                         CIP
                                          AC

CONTENTS

BLIZZARDS

WHAT DOES THE WORD BLIZZARD MAKE YOU THINK OF? School closings? Jammed roadways? Fresh powder for skiing? Big drifts perfect for sledding?

Blizzards mean different things to different people. For snow plowers, blizzards mean lots of work and little sleep. For some travelers, blizzards mean delays and detours. For other travelers, blizzards mean canceled vacations. For drivers, blizzards mean slow traffic, closed roads and car accidents. For some unlucky people, blizzards mean death.

A blizzard strikes New York City.

A blizzard is a vicious act of nature. During a blizzard, strong winds pick up snow. The snow may already be on the ground, or the snow may be falling. The wind blows the snow violently, making it very hard for a person to see. Everything looks white. Drivers are blinded. Chain-reaction car crashes occur in whiteout situations. In extreme whiteout conditions, a person's depth perception can be altered. An object such as a pail may appear to be a building.

Not all snowstorms are blizzards. The National Weather Service says that a snowstorm is not a blizzard until winds blow a large amount of snow 35 or more miles per hour (56 kph). In addition,

4

The Washington Monument
is obscured as a blizzard
blankets Washington, D.C.

Cars are immobilized in Chicago, Illinois, after a 20-inch (51-cm) snowfall.

visibility must be less than 500 feet (152 m). The worst kind of blizzard is called a severe blizzard. The winds of a severe blizzard travel more than 45 miles per hour (72 kph). Visibility in a severe blizzard is near zero percent.

The most common places for blizzards to occur are the northern Great Plains, the prairie provinces of Canada, the upper Mississippi Valley, and the eastern Arctic. There are no natural boundaries, like mountains or volcanoes, protecting these areas from strong winds. This makes it easier for winds to pick up snow. Blizzards are less common in areas where a mountain cuts down the amount of wind.

If it's the middle of winter, and the weather seems unusually warm, watch out! Blizzards often follow warm winter weather. A blizzard works like this:

1) A cold mass of air moves out of the Arctic.

2) The cold air mass moves into a Temperate Zone.

3) The heavy, cold air makes

the warm air in the Temperate Zone rise.

4) The warm air rises to the boundary between the cold and warm air. The boundary is called a cold front.

5) The rising action causes a heavy snowstorm. Cold north winds come with the snowstorm.

Blizzards have been haunting humans for a very long time. Over the years, people have developed different ways of coping. Farmers used to tie ropes from their houses to their barns so they wouldn't become lost in the deep snow-drifts. Sometimes the ropes didn't help. Fine, powdery snow can choke the lungs. If a lot of snow is blowing very hard, snow can cause a person to suffocate to death.

Midwestern historians tell us about farmers found just inches from their doors, frozen to death. Sometimes, bodies of blizzard victims are not found until spring, when the tall snow banks finally melt.

A farmer drives his cows to the barn during a blizzard.

ICE AND SNOW

BLIZZARDS DO NOT OCCUR IN ALL PARTS OF THE WORLD. The same type of snow and ice do not fall in all parts of the world, either. The kind of snow and ice you see falling outside your window depends on where you live.

In coastal areas, snow is usually wet and heavy. Snowballs and snowmen pack hard. In the plains, snow is usually dry and light, like powder. The snow in the plains is picked up more easily by winds than the snow in the coastal areas. It makes sense, then, that blizzards are more common in the plains.

Blowing snow forms drifts. During heavy winds, some spots on the ground may have many feet of snow. Other areas may only have a few inches. A low drift is a drift that is two to four feet (.6 to 1.2 m) high. A high drift is a drift that is over an adult's head. Blizzards often form high drifts.

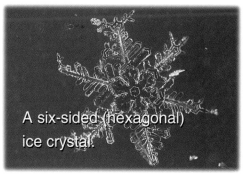

A six-sided (hexagonal) ice crystal.

Regardless of what type of snow or ice falls, the start of the precipitation process is much the same. All snow and ice start as water molecules inside a cloud. When the air is cold enough, the water freezes into ice particles. The ice particles organize themselves into hexagons, which have six sides. If the ice particles continue to gather more ice particles, they can grow to be many-sided figures.

How big and detailed an ice particle gets depends upon the tem-

Winds whipping across the prairie create snowdrift patterns.

perature. At 30°F (-1°C) ice particles grow into thin plates. At 15°F (-9°C) the particles grow into hollow columns. At 5°F (-15°C) ice particles grow into the classic snowflake. "Classic" snowflakes are more detailed than other kinds of snowflakes.

No two snowflakes are the same. Because each ice crystal experiences different air temperatures and different air currents as it falls to the earth, there are an infinite number of snowflake patterns. The beautiful snowflake patterns shown on holiday paper are not very common. Over 99 percent of snow crystals are asymmetrical—most snowflakes look as if they were put together haphazardly. The sides are uneven. One edge may jut out far from the rest. Many snowflakes do not look like snowflakes at all. They look like clumps of sugar.

At any given time, snow covers one-fourth of the world. Some areas like Antarctica and the far north have snow all year round. People who live in cold climates have adapted their lifestyle around cold, snow, and ice.

For thousands of years, the Inuit have lived in the far north. They know all about cold, freezing temperatures and blinding snow.

Today, many Inuit live in wood houses. Others still build warm shelters out of snow and ice. A dome-shaped snow house is called an igloo. To an outsider, the vast distances of white look deserted of all life. Not to the Inuit. The Inuit know where to find Arctic animals' favorite spots.

Inuits have survived for a long time in the harsh cold because they have adapted so well to the environment. They can read directions by looking at snowdrifts. They can predict blizzards by looking at the sky. Snow and ice are critical to the Inuit way of life. They have over 40 different words for "snow."

Inuit children in winter furs.

An igloo with snowshoes outside.

Downtown New York City
during the Blizzard of 1888.

BLIZZARDS OF THE PAST

THE MORNING OF JANUARY 12, 1888, WAS ALMOST LIKE any other morning in the Dakotas and Nebraska. It may have been a little warmer than usual. It may have been a little brighter than usual. One thing is certain. There was no evidence of the sky's impending doom.

Children walked off to school under the sun's bright rays. Farmers milked cows and fed livestock. Farmers' wives probably baked, washed clothes, or gathered eggs from the chicken coop. It seemed like any other winter morning. But it wasn't. In just a few hours, hundreds of people would be dead.

People struggling to walk in New York City during the Blizzard of 1888.

The 1888 blizzard was sudden and violent. Stories of the blizzard have been passed down through families. One survivor remembered it vividly. He was playing outside (in short sleeves!) during recess, when he glanced at the sky.

"Something coming rolling toward us with great fury from the northwest, and making a loud noise. It looked like a long string of big bales of cotton, each one bound tightly with heavy cords of silver, and then all tied together with great silvery ropes."

The boy warned his teacher, and they hurried to safety inside the school. Other people weren't as lucky. Some parents came looking for their children, only to get lost in the blizzard and die.

Animals that didn't make it into barns froze to death. The blizzard is sometimes referred to as the "Schoolchildren's Blizzard."

That same year, a terrible blizzard struck the East Coast. One fourth of the American population was affected by what came to be known as "The Blizzard of '88." From March 12 through March 14, cities from Maine to Maryland came to a standstill as the storm brought 40 to 50 inches (102 to 127 cm) of snow. Transportation ceased. Communication stopped. Businesses shut down. People hardly left their homes. In New York City, winds of up to 48 miles per hour (77 kph) were reported.

In New England, people looked out their windows to see 40 foot (12 m) snowdrifts. The storm claimed nearly 400 lives, including 200 in New York City alone.

The "Blizzard of '88" also went out to sea. Sailors reported winds of up to 90 miles per hour (145 kph). Waves were three stories high! The blizzard destroyed about 200 ships and claimed about 100 sailors' lives.

In 1997, a mighty blizzard wreaked havoc on Colorado. Eight-foot (2.4 m) snowdrifts hit some areas. Schools and businesses closed. Roads closed. Denver International Airport and Colorado Springs Airport both closed.

Snowdrifts form on the wind-swept Midwestern plains.

From January 6-8, 1996, the "Blizzard of '96" and ensuing flooding killed 187 people and caused nearly $3 billion in total damages.

THE BLIZZARD
OF 1996

| 1-6 | 6-12 | 12-24 | 24-36 | 36-48 |

SNOWFALL (IN INCHES)

Thousands of travelers were stranded.

Visibility was so poor that cars smashed into everything: cars, trees, buildings, road signs. Some cars slid into ditches. Many parts of the state shut down. Rescue trucks tried to get through to accident scenes. There was so much snow that it took some ambulances hours to reach people.

In Pueblo, power was off for days. With no heat and no light, some families had to leave their homes to live in emergency shelters. Schools closed. Some kids climbed up to the top of snowdrifts. Other kids sought ways to earn extra money by shoveling walks and brushing off cars.

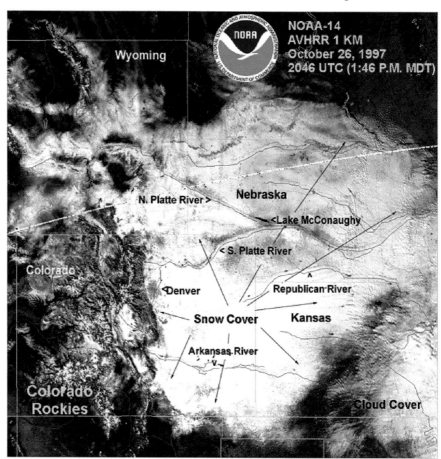

This satellite image from the National Oceanic & Atmospheric Administration shows the snowfall pattern after the blizzard of October 1997.

A car tries to navigate an icy road after a blizzard in Minneapolis, Minnesota.

INSIDE A BLIZZARD

Wind speeds in a blizzard reach 35 miles per hour (56 kph) or greater.

Visibility in a blizzard is less than 500 feet (152 m). Traffic accidents often occur due to poor visibility.

Cold, moist air forms six-sided ice crystals, which bunch together and fall to the ground as snowflakes.

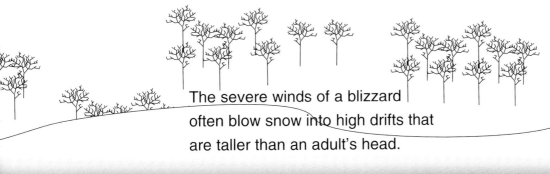

The severe winds of a blizzard often blow snow into high drifts that are taller than an adult's head.

An iceberg floats at the edge of
an approaching blizzard in the
Gerlache Straits, Antarctica.

ANTARCTIC BLIZZARDS

BLIZZARDS BRING BLINDING WHITEOUTS, FREEZING temperatures, and huge snowdrifts to many people's homes. Do the blizzards we see seem unbearable? Can you imagine anything worse? Try. The blizzards in the Antarctic are far worse.

Antarctica is full of ice and snow all year round. In some parts, the ice on Antarctica is two miles (3.2 km) thick. The South Pole is almost exactly in the center of Antarctica. If you stood on the South Pole, you would see very little except miles and miles of ice and snow. To some people the patterns in the snow remind them of the ocean. The hard ridges carved in the snow by wind are called sastrugi. Sastrugi make wave-like patterns on the snow.

Antarctica is one of the seven continents. It is larger than the United States. No one lives on Antarctica because of the extreme

A man tries to secure a rope near his tent at a camp on Butson Point, a glacier in northeast Antarctica.

temperatures and the shifting of the ice and snow.

Antarctica's winds are very powerful. Wind gusts of up to 120 miles per hour (193 kph) are common. Blowing snow is so strong that it has been known to blow Antarctic explorers off their feet!

The windiest place on earth is Cape Denison, Antarctica. The average wind speed is 50 miles per hour (80 kph). The average wind speed in the United States is about 10 miles per hour (16 kph), five times less than at Cape Denison.

Cape Denison claims the earth's fiercest blizzards. In Antarctica, blizzards occur 10 to 12 times every year. They usually last for several days. Whirlwinds can pick up objects weighing hundreds of pounds, whirl them around and then fling them down again.

Many explorers have studied Antarctica and its blizzards. Some have died in the process. Others have lived to tell us of their experiences. Richard Byrd spent one winter alone deep in the Antarctic interior. He wrote about a blizzard he experienced:

"It is a queer experience to watch a blizzard rise. First there is the wind, rising out of nowhere. . . sometimes, if the wind strikes hard the drift comes across the barrier like a hurrying white cloud, tossed hundreds of feet in the air. Other times the growth is gradual. You become conscious of a general slithering movement on all sides. The air fills with tiny scraping and sliding and rustling sounds as the first loose crystals stir. In a little while they are moving as solidly as an incoming tide, which creams over the ankles, then surges to the waist, and finally is at the throat. I have walked in drift so thick as not to be able to see a foot ahead of me. . . The noise was as if the entire physical world were tearing itself to pieces. . . To see was impossible. Millions of tiny pellets exploded in my eyes, stinging like BB shot. It was even hard to breathe, because snow instantly clogged the mouth and nostrils. I made my way. . . on hands and knees, scared that I might be bowled off my feet if I stood erect; one false step and I should be lost forever."

TRACKING BLIZZARDS

IN THE PAST, THERE WERE VERY FEW WAYS OF MAKING accurate weather predictions. As the unlucky victims of the "Schoolchildren's Blizzard" of 1888 learned, weather can change fast—sometimes with deadly results.

During the 1800s, meteorologists used simple instruments and the naked eye to forecast the weather. Meteorologists did not have a way to measure what clouds and winds were doing far above the ground. Even if meteorologists in the 1800s correctly predicted a blizzard, the number of people they could warn was limited. There were no cars, no telephones, and no televisions.

Today's meteorologists have more ways of accurately predicting all kinds of weather, including blizzards. Today's meteorologists have special tools that show them what the weather is doing high above in the earth's atmosphere. The two main tools that

meteorologists use are radar and satellites. If you watch the local news, you will probably see pictures from a radar screen. Radar uses radio waves to locate storms and clouds. Weather satellites take photographs of earth from space. Satellites help scientists and meteorologists watch a storm system make its way around the world. By

A meteorologist with the National Weather Service tracks a storm.

knowing ahead what the weather system looks like, meteorologists can warn people about upcoming weather through radio and television. Every day people turn on the news to get the latest forecast.

Does it look like snow to you? Turn on your television and look to see if the National Weather Service has issued any warnings. When a winter storm looks dangerous, the National Weather Service announces winter weather advisories. The advisories are usually announced 12 to 36 hours before the weather is predicted to hit. By announcing the weather in advance, people can prepare for the worst.

The National Weather Service issues three main winter weather warnings. A winter storm watch is issued when heavy snow is expected, and icy conditions are possible. If it looks as if the weather will definitely hit the area, the National Weather Service may change the winter storm watch to a winter storm warning. If the storm does hit a certain area and it continues to bring heavy snow for more than three hours and visibility is poor, the National Weather Service will issue a blizzard warning. For a blizzard warning to be issued, visibility must be less than a quarter of a mile (.4 km).

It is important to keep tuned to the weather at all times, especially in winter. Being informed may save your life. People are not always close to a radio or television. If you are a hunter, hiker, or other outdoor adventurer you should keep in mind the warning signs of a blizzard:

1) The barometric pressure drops slightly.

2) Cloud cover thickens.

3) The sky appears leaden.

4) Snow may fall, but not heavily at first.

5) Weather seems unusually warm.

6) During the night, the temperature drops by as much as 50°F (10°C).

7) The north wind seems strong.

8) More snow falls.

9) Wind speed increases dramatically, and starts to pick up the snow from the ground.

If the above things happen, a blizzard may be heading your way.

STAYING SAFE

HUMANS ARE NOT POLAR BEARS. HUMANS ARE NOT MADE to endure very cold temperatures. Polar bears have thick, heavy fur to keep them warm. Humans have very little body hair.

From the very beginning, people have worn protective clothing in cold temperatures. Most people used to wear animal skins. Today, in many parts of the world, animal skins have been replaced by thinner, layered clothing and padded jackets filled with wool or down feathers.

By preparing ahead for blizzard conditions, you will reduce the likelihood of being a victim to winter's worst fury. Proper clothing and common sense will help a great deal in battling cold temperatures and dire conditions.

Wearing warm clothes in winter is very important to help your body fight off frostbite and hypothermia. When fingers, toes, and faces are exposed to extreme cold, frostbite occurs. Arteries and veins start to close. Blood is no longer being pumped into the frostbitten

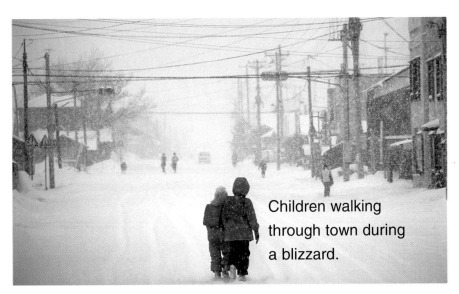

Children walking through town during a blizzard.

area. In a short amount of time, the exposed skin feels numb. The area becomes white and waxy looking. If you notice this, gently rub the area with a warm hand. Untreated frostbite can result in losing fingers, toes, or other body parts.

Hypothermia occurs when your body temperature falls. A normal human body temperature is close to 98.6°F (37°C). When your body temperature drops, you start to shiver. Shivering is your body's way of generating heat. If you start to shiver, walk around, jump, or do something else to generate heat. If a person's body temperature drops to 89.6°F (32°C), violent shaking and shivering occur. Shivering uses a lot of energy. If you are shivering, get out of the cold as soon as possible.

If a person shivers for a long period of time, they become lethargic and ready to sleep. If this happens, get out of the cold. If you are stranded outside, do not go to sleep! Try to build a shelter away from the wind and cold. Try to build a small fire. If there is more

than one person, huddle together. Brush the snow off your clothes before it melts. It is much harder to warm up in wet clothes than dry clothes.

When body temperatures fall even more, muscles no longer work together. At this point, the victim does not think clearly. The victim may not even appear to notice that he or she is in danger. After a while, a person will lose consciousness. The heart will eventually stop beating.

Using your common sense will save you from many winter dilemmas. If a blizzard is forecast, stay home. Do not go outside. Do not travel. Road conditions can change for the worse in a matter of seconds. If you are traveling, stop at the nearest building to seek shelter. Always keep extra bright clothes and a winter safety kit in the car. The winter safety kit should include non-perishable food items, a flashlight with extra batteries, a can and waterproof matches (to melt snow for drinking water) and a compass.

AFTER THE STORM

BLIZZARDS CAN BE A FEW HOURS LONG, OR THEY CAN last several days. The intensity of the blizzard will determine what hazards lie ahead after the storm is over. The day after a blizzard could mean business as usual. Schools may be open. Stores may be open. Everything could be back to normal. The only reminder of the blizzard may be the snowdrifts left outside.

On the other hand, blizzards may cause more lasting delays. Schools and stores may still be closed. Watch your local news or listen to the local radio station to find out.

Blizzards can cause severe damage to personal property. Heavy snow on roofs can cause major roof damage, some of which can be very bad. You may have to vacate your house until it's fixed.

Plows clearing a mountain road.

Blizzards cause car accidents. People flock to the repair shops on the days following a blizzard. Being without a car could be an inconvenience to your family.

The power could go off during and after a blizzard. Usually a power cut-off is caused by heavy snow and ice on power lines. Depending on where you live, lack of power may mean that you have to leave your home for a short while. Most communities set up shelters. Shelters are temporary places to live while things at home get better. Most shelters do not allow pets. Don't worry. During severe weather, you can take your pet to an animal shelter. Animal shelters will take good care of your pet until you can return home.

Roads may still not be safe on the days following a blizzard. Heavy snow and ice may be packed into the road. Getting from one place to another may take much longer than usual. Some roads may be closed.

After a blizzard it is important to restock your winter safety kits. Make sure that everything is replaced. If you used the spare batteries for the flashlight, make sure to add another set.

Blizzards bring many dangers, but they also bring snow fun. More snow means more snowmen, more sledding, and more skiing. When you go to play outside always remember to tell someone where you're going. Many people have been lost in the huge snowdrifts left behind from a blizzard. Also be sure to wear bright clothes. Bright clothes shout, "Watch out! Here I come!"

Snowplows clearing the streets of New York City.

INTERNET SITES

http://www.usatoday.com

Go to WEATHER. Check out more about blizzards, winter storms, or any kind of weather.

http://cirrus.sprl.umich.edu/wenet/

Check out the weather forecast in your city. Get snapshots of weather through live weather cams.

http://weathereye.kgan.com

Do you think you know what to do in a blizzard? Test your skills in the game "Blizzard Attack."

These sites are subject to change. Go to your favorite search engine and type in "blizzards" for more sites.

PASS IT ON

Science buffs: educate readers around the country by passing on information you've learned about blizzards. Share your little-known facts and interesting stories. We want to hear from you!

To get posted on the ABDO Publishing Company Web site, E-mail us at "Science@abdopub.com"

Visit the ABDO Publishing Company Web site at:
www.abdopub.com

GLOSSARY

Asymmetrical: Not the same on all sides.

Barometric pressure: Air pressure.

Cold front: The boundary made when a cold air mass pushes up against a warm air mass.

Fahrenheit: A temperature measurement.

Frostbite: The destruction of skin tissue caused by exposure to temperatures of extreme cold.

High drift: A snowdrift that is taller than an adult.

Hypothermia: The lowering of body temperature; it can cause death in some instances.

Interior: The inside part.

Low drift: A snowdrift that is about 2 to 4 feet (.6 to 1.2 m) high.

Meteorologist: A person who predicts and studies weather.

National Weather Service: The service that collects weather statistics and issues storm warnings.

Non-perishable: A food item that will not spoil.

Precipitation: Liquid or frozen water that falls from the sky.

Sastrugi: Ridges in the Antarctic snow carved by strong wind.

Visibility: How far you can see.

Whiteout: When snow cover becomes so thick that it makes it very hard to see.

A truck stuck in a snowdrift after a blizzard.

INDEX